# Guided Meditations for Mindfulness and Self Healing

*Follow Beginners Meditation Scripts for Anxiety and Stress Relief, Deep Sleep, Panic Attacks, Depression, Relaxation and More for a Happier Life!*

By Healing Meditation Academy

# Table of Contents

## Guided Meditations for Mindfulness and Self Healing
## Chapter 1: Mindfulness Meditation

Beginner Breathing (10 minutes if done individually)

The Stimulating Breath: The aim here is to enhance your overall alertness and internal energy sources.
The 4-7-8 Exercise

Breathing Exercise Three:

Breathe Counting
Anger Relaxation
Grief Relaxation

## Chapter 2: Chakra Healing Meditation

Root Chakra Meditation (Meditation time approx. 15 when repeated 2 times)

Root (2)

Sacral Chakra Meditation (Meditation time approx. 15 when repeated 2 times)

Sacral Chakra (2)

Solar Plexus Meditation (Meditation time approx. 15 when repeated 3 times)

Solar Plexus (2)

Heart Chakra Meditation (Meditation time approx. 15 when repeated 2 times)

> Heart (2)

Throat Chakra Meditation (Meditation time approx. 15 when repeated 3 times)

> Throat (2)

Third Eye Chakra Meditation (Meditation time approx. 15 when repeated 2 times)

> Third eye (2)

Crown Chakra Meditation (Meditation time approx. 10 when repeated 3 times)

> Body Scan (10 mins. Repeat 5x)

# Chapter 1: Mindfulness Meditation

## Beginner Breathing (10 minutes if done individually)

**The Stimulating Breath: The aim here is to enhance your overall alertness and internal energy sources.**

- Begin by first inhaling and then exhaling in a rapid manner through your nostrils. Remember to keep your mouth completely closed but still very relaxed. Ensure that your breathing is exactly equal in its duration while making sure that the breaths are short. You will find that this particular exercise is rather loud.

- Aim for around 3 inhales and exhales each second. This will create a very sharp movement of your diaphragm— similar to a bellows. After each individual breathing cycle, you can start to breathe normally for a short period of around 1 minute.

- On your very first attempt, refrain from doing this for more than 20 seconds. You can, however, increase your time by the duration of 5 seconds until a full minute has been reached. After a while of performing this exercise, you will likely feel boosts of energy and awareness similar to a great workout.

## The 4-7-8 Exercise

Begin by sitting with your back completely straight. Then, place this tip of the tongue along with the tissue that sits right behind the upper portion of your front teeth— hold it here for the duration of the exercise. This exercise will require that you exhale through your mouth and around the tongue. If the movement is too awkward, you can also purse your lips for added comfort.

- Exhale all the way through your mouth, creating a whooshing noise.

- Next, inhale silently after closing your mouth. Inhale through your nose for a total duration of 4 seconds.

- Ensure that your breath is held for a period of 7 seconds.

- Now, begin to exhale with a whooshing noise through your mouth for 8 seconds.

- This counts as one cycle of breathing. Now, you are to inhale once again and restart the original cycle. Do this 3 times totaling 4 breaths.
Keeping mind that this breathing excursive requires that you

continually inhale through the nose and exhale through the mouth. Make sure that your tongue is kept in the same position at all times during the exercise. Also, you will notice that exhaling will last nearly twice the amount of time as inhaling will. However, the total amount of time that is spent during each breathing sessions is not of integral importance just as long as you remember the 4:7:8 ratios.

## Breathing Exercise Three:

### Breathe Counting

Perform this meditative exercise for 10-15 minutes per session. This time is preferred because it allows you to fully garner all of the best benefits that mindfulness meditation has to offer. However, if you are pressed for time, you will find that even a few minutes will carry many benefits for you as well.

- Sit in a comfortable position with your back completely straight and your head leaning forward.

- Start to shut your eyes and inhale slowly and deeply.

- Next, exhale slowly without being too forceful. You want this rhythm to be slow and quiet, but it is okay if these vary for you.

- Acknowledge incoming thoughts even if they are plentiful. Let go of them and return to your breath as soon as you recognize that you have become distracted.

- Start conducting a full scan of your body from the top of your head down to your feet.

- Notice any subtle or strong sensations in all of the areas that you scan.

- As you move along your body and begin to notice sensations, recognize them and let go. The goal is only to heighten awareness of these sensations, rather than trying to change them.

- Now, count "one" when you exhale. Remember to release your breath very slowly and at a measured pace.

- Next, count "two"... continues sequentially to a count of five totals.

- Once you have reached a count of five, restart the cycle by counting "one" for the next exhale.

- Be sure to refrain from counting any higher than 5 once you exhale. If your count reaches beyond 5, this is a clear indication of your attention having wondered.

In this next module for mindfulness meditation, we will tackle pain management. I will guide you along with a session designed to have you concentrate on acceptance and observation. In this way, you will be able to morph all of your pain, and then focus your mind during the meditation exercise to install both mental and physical calm and relief from pain.

- So, start by finding and settling into a comfortable position ensuring that your back has enough support. While you are laying on your back, or if you are seated in a chair with enough support for your head, you can begin this session.

- As you come to settle yourself, take notice of how your body and mind feel in this unique moment. Remember, you do not need to attempt to change anything at this moment. Simply become a patient, calm and distant observer of your physical and mental state. Managing pain starts with simple and calm observation.

- Now, notice where some of your pain and tension is being carried. Where is the pain in your body? Which parts of your body are calm and at ease?

- Start conducting a full scan of your body from the top of your head down to your feet.

- Notice any subtle or strong sensations in all of the areas that you scan.
- As you move along your body and begin to notice sensations, recognize them and let go. The goal is only to heighten awareness of these sensations, rather than trying to change them.
- Take another deep inhaling breath... then release your breath through a calm and slow exhale.

- Breath in again....now breath out.

- Keep breathing... slowly... calmly.

- Now, conduct another scan of your body:

Feel the soles of your feet on the floor

Feel the cold air inhaled through your nostrils

Notice any unique bodily sensations that you are feeling

When you are distracted or lost in thought, bring your attention right back to your breath

Feel the rise and fall of your chest as you inhale and exhale

Feel and notice where the movement of your breath is felt in your body

Notice the influx of thoughts and then return to a bodily sensation or the breath

Notice where your body is uneasy or uncomfortable

Notice whether your breaths are shallow or deep without changing them

Feel the cold air moving through your nostrils and filling your chest causing it to expand.

Let go of any pain that you feel move along your body. Do not judge your pain or sensations, whether they are positive or negative, just be at peace and passive accept them.

## Anger Relaxation

- Start by finding and settling into a comfortable position ensuring that your back has enough support. While you are laying on your back, or if you are seated in a chair with enough support for your head, you can begin this session.

- Where is your tension being held in your body?
- Where, if anywhere, is the pain located in your body?
- Is any part of your body totally relaxed?
- Now, perform a full body scan from the top of your head to the soles of your feet.
- Breath in... and breath out now.
- Focus on your breath, bringing its rhythm to a smooth flow in and out of your mouth with no rush.
- Now, keep going onward with the

management of your pain through relaxation breathing. There is no need to force anything to take place; just notice how your body is feeling, without judgment, or negativity. If you begin to have negative thoughts and feelings, bring your focus right back to your breath. Just passively observe.

- Keep observing the state of your discomfort and pain-free from judgment. Your body is constantly changing, feeling one way at one moment, and another the next.

- This moment to moment state of change is constant. Simply observe each and every moment as it comes and passes ever so peacefully.

- While all of our pain is not wanted

and hard to cope with, try to focus on your pain with an aura of acceptance and peace. Free from judgment and pain.

Accept and be at peace with how you feel emotionally and physically. Resistance is the cause of suffering and discomfort.

- Accepting and observing are key to moving beyond your pain and anger, and allowing yourself to step into peace and acceptance.
- Focus on simply allowing your body, mind, and spirit to just... be. Be still and at total ease— whether you feel positively or negatively.
- Repeat. I totally accept all of myself. I love who I am.
- I fully accept the pain that I am

feeling.
- I completely release the need that I have for control over how I feel and judgment for the way that I feel.
- I accept all aspects of who I am with love and peace ... free of pain and judgment.
- When distracted bring all of your focus directly back to your breath once again.

When you feel ready, bring all of your attention to the sounds of your surroundings... slowly; when you are ready... open your eyes. Refreshed and awakened, you are free to move through your day at ease and peace.

## Grief Relaxation

Relax in a comfortable position. You can be seated or on the floor. Whichever bests suits you at the present moment. Just be... Allow your thoughts, however urgent and furious they enter your mind, to simply pass through your mind with calmness and acceptance.

Focus on your breath, bringing in the deep, cool air that fills your lungs. Now, exhale slowly and peacefully. Do this 3 more times; each time bring all of your focus to your breath calmly and with ease. Fully immerse yourself into this present moment of calm and wellness.

Now, begin observing your present thoughts. Notice any particular thoughts about your pain and grief. Are there thoughts of loss? Do you feel as though you want to change these thoughts? Fight against the temptation to change these thoughts. Simply allows them to flow into your mind, and simply label them as "grief" or "loss" or "pain."

Notice that when you simply label these thoughts, there is a sudden distance that you have created from them. Indeed, these are not who you truly are. They are just ephemeral thoughts.

After labeling these thoughts, bring

your attention back to your breath once again. Inhaling and exhaling with calm ease. Notice the coolness of the air coming into your nostrils and leaving out of your mouth.

Now, focus on the areas of discomfort in your body. Imagine an altered sensation; this can be whichever sensation or feeling that you choose to experience. You might also want to feel a nice tingle along your leg or forearm. This will give you added control over your physical sensations, even if just for a fleeting moment.

Now, feel this sensation in full. Feel it replacing your feelings and thoughts of having lost somebody or something. Allow this sensation to replace your pain and grief. More and more, one bit at a time, allow your grief to go away.

This sensation will allow you to relax and let go of your grief. This distance is healthy and peaceful for you. Now, take a deep inhale... now breath out. In and out... once again... in and out. The cool air is a calming sensation for your body, mind, and spirit.

Embrace the energy of passively accepting your feelings and thoughts. Simply allow yourself to fully embrace how you are feeling and whichever emotional, mental and physical state that you are in at this present moment.

Breath in calmly and slowly; inhaling and exhaling. Allow yourself to be an observer of every breath and let your breathing be deep and peaceful. Embrace calmness and wholeness with each and every one of your breaths.

Be aware of all that your senses perceive at the present moment in time. Focus on one thought at a time, and label them.

Notice each sound that comes to your ears. Feel how your clothes sit on your body again. Just observe without feeling as though you have to change something.

Now, in closing, scan your body from the top of your head to the soles of your feet. Allow all of your physical sensations along the way to be fully embraced without judgment or a need to change them. Peacefully move along your body.

When you have reached your feet, bring your attention to your breath one last time. Inhale and exhale slowly and peacefully... when you are ready...

Open your eyes.

# Chapter 2: Chakra Healing Meditation

## Root Chakra Meditation (Meditation time approx. 15 when repeated 2 times)

Officially, the name of the first chakra is actually, Muladhara, and is derived from two words: Mula, meaning root, and Dhara— meaning support. The main role of this particular chakra is to connect the entirety of your energy with that of the Earth. This exercise is called grounding. When considering the Root Chakra, you should consider this as day-to-day survival on earth.

Moreover, the central role of this energy is to provide you with all that you need to survive and live a fruitful life here on earth. In today's current society and time period, this idea tends to manifest as emotional as well as financial security.

Now...

Be comfortable. If your body is lying on the floor, allow your entire body to relax and feel comfortable fully. If sitting, allow your hands to be relaxed on your thighs or just resting on our side. Either posture is fine.

Now, shut your eyes. This time is perfectly laid out for you. Let all of your anxieties go. Let your spirit flow beautifully into the present moment. This current moment is all that exists; there is no past, no future; neither exists. Only the present moment is here now.

Let your shoulders rest and drop. Allow your hands to rest completely. Let your body, in its full form, become soft and settle naturally. Let your face be fully calm, as well as your eyes, and hair. Unclench your jaw and allow your body's muscles to ease fully. Become soft.

Take in a clean breath; this will cleanse your spirit and allow you to relax. Let go of all of the tension in your body. Let your breathing to settle with a natural motion naturally. Resist the temptation to control your breath. Just be an observer of your breath, thoughts, and emotions. Breath in, breath out; observe the rhythm of the breath. Just observe.

Now, bring your mind's attentiveness and energy to the spine's base. Visualize a small red light, swirling in a circle, almost like a small whirlpool. Just observe and notice how it feels and looks. Acquire a keen sense of how your breath is functioning. What speed is the breath? Is it accelerated or is it slower? Breathe in and breathe out all of the tension within your body and spirit. Now breathe the red light into your body. Feel this air in the Base Chakra. Observe the red light filling the Base Chakra and spreading outwardly. Breathe in while attracting the red light closer to you. Feel the warmth of this red light. Breathe in and breathe out the tension. Slowly repeat without judgment but as an observer.

The red light attracts with it health, strength and a strong sense of security. When this red light fills you, allow it to spread to your feet, feel the empowerment that the light brings as it fully connects with the energy of the earth. Feel the calm and relaxing energy of the red light. Breathe in the earth's fresh and calming energy.

Breath into your body personal security, self-confidence, and breath out ever fear within your spirit. Remind yourself that you are fully safe, secure and in touch with your spirit.

Now it is time to close this chakra. Bring all of your attention to the small red light that rests at the Base Chakra. Visualize this light becoming smaller, bringing it all the way down to the size of a thimble. Now, begin the mantra, The Base Chakra is functioning with complete normality." "My spirit now has an approach to my earthly needs that is balanced and calm. Every single need of mine is fully cared for."

Bring all of your awareness to the incoming and outgoing flow of the breath. Breathe in and breathe out. Feel the cool breathing as it enters your nostrils and flows all the way down to the back of the throat and all the way into the full expansion of your lungs. Be aware of the natural movement of the stomach as it expands and contracts. Feel your body resting against the floor. Feel your fingers, shrug the shoulders. When you are completely ready, calmly open your eyes.

## Root (2)

Take a long, drawn out deep breath. When you exhale, adjust your attention to your spinal base. Now, visualize a red chakra that is shining brightly. The warmth and glow of this chakra relaxes your mind and heart, allowing you to fully feel the safety and serenity that this chakra brings.

Feel grounded and unshaken as if you are a massive rock that is held warmly by the earth. Visualize yourself standing calmly at the base of a snowy mountain that is lifting itself upward toward the sky. Right in front of you is a massive opening that leads to a cave. The suns's rays enter in an inviting way as you walk into the cave.

Take a step forward and walk inside the cave. You will see that the cave is surrounded by smooth walls and a ceiling that extends very high. There is a warm, soft and gentle breeze that allows you to feel comfortable. Walk a little farther and be aware of your surroundings.

You now notice a path that has opened into a big, circular room. There is a large rectangular rock sitting in the middle. A small and warm ray of sun is slipping through a tiny fissure in the ceiling and bathes the stone with a glow of warmth.

Walk over to the rock and take a seat on it. Sit cross-legged- this will come naturally to you.

You now start to feel as though you are an appendage of the mountain- as though you are a piece of it. You feel anchored very deeply connected to the earth. You are safe. You can see that the earth is nourishing and supporting every aspect of your being.

Now you can see that your first chakra is spinning and beginning to gain strength. As this chakra starts to spin much faster, a red light spans over you and enters every single feel in your body, and even every pore.

Allow the calm from your surrounding see into your body and spirit, enhancing your peace and inner serenity.

Take a deep breath and allow yourself to feel the energy that has funnelled to the bottom of your spine. Hold onto this feeling of high energy for an extended period, becoming filled with good energy and peace. Now, once your feel filled with the great energy of this state, let go of this feeling and focus your attention on your breath, breathing in slowly and exhaling in the same way.

Relax within this state of awareness. This awareness will lead you toward your very best self. You are stronger, calmer and more peaceful than ever before.

Now, rise in a gentle manner, and walk out of the room, through the path to the outside of the cave. Take a gaze back at the mountain and feel connected to it— as though you are one with it.

Once you are ready, you can open your eyes and rise.

# Sacral Chakra Meditation (Meditation time approx. 15 when repeated 2 times)

This second chakra knows as the sacral chakra or svadhishana translates directly to "the place of the self." Notably, this chakra is most concerned with one's identity as a human being and how one is to deal with it. Perhaps the most beneficial aspect of this chakra is that it provides one with creative energy to maximize their enjoyment of life.

Get yourself into a comfortable position. If you are laying on the floor, allow your entire body to fully relax and become comfortable. If you are sitting in a chair, settle your hands on your thighs or at the side of your body.

Now, close your eyes. This time if uniquely set out for you. Leave all of your worries. Let them go.

Have awareness for all of the sounds that surround you; just allow them to be present without judgment or interaction.

Be aware of the shade and light permeating through your eyelids. Feel the soft cool air softly touching your body's surface.

Sense the massive sky above you, along with the broad horizons that stretch around you, feel the earth below you, supporting your weight and body.

Draw in a breath that cleanses you and then breath out all of the tension that has built up inside of your body and mind. Let your breath fall naturally into a rhythm.

When your thoughts arise and begin to distract you, just gently bring your attention back to your breath. Breathe in and breathe out with awareness.

Now, draw your attention to your abdomen. Visualize a beautiful orange light that is swirling in a way that is similar to a small pool. Be aware of how this feels, what does it look like? What is the function of this light? Is there a tingling feeling? Gently notice the thoughts in your mind, how fast are they? Are they troubling you? Can you visualize the orange color within your mind?

Bring your attention back to your breath now. Breathe in calm, breath out resistance and tension. Now breathe into yourself the orange light of warm. Notice how this light is breathed into your abdomen area—directly into your Sacral Chakra. Allow this energy to spread outward to your surroundings, sending love and positivity.

Kindly welcome all of the pleasureful dealings that this orange light brings. Breath in joy and breath out all of the tension inside of you (Repeat in rhythm).

Now, it is time to close this chakra down. Bring all of your attention to your abdomen, to the orange light of the Sacral Chakra. Notice this light getting smaller, all the way down to the small size of a fairy's light. Bring this light into normal function. Repeat the mantra, "My Sacral Chakra has begun operating normally."

Draw your awareness to the soft, cool flow of your breath. Breathe in and out in a repeated rhythm. Be aware of the cool air as it enters your nostrils and down the throat, filling your lungs fully. Let yourself notice the natural and soft motion of your stomach when you inhale and exhale. Rest in awareness as your entire body is resting against the floor, or in your chair. Bring all of your attention to your hands and move them slowly. Feel the physical sensation of this motion. Shrug your shoulders and drop them slowly if they are tense. Feel the temperature of the room, and hear all of the sounds that are nearby.

When you are fully ready, open your eyes and rise slowly.

## Sacral Chakra (2)

Get into a comfortable position. Either on the floor or seated gently in a chair. Your hands in your lap and feet on the floor.

Notice your physical sensations, followed by resting in awareness of the sounds around you and the temperature in the room that you are in.

Now, invite in the orange color of the setting sun. Allow yourself to be encompassed by your Hara, with orange light being the source of empowerment, balance, and motivation. Feed your Hara and repeat the mantra, "I will honor all of my sacred personal needs." "I hereby will allow my spirit to be fully nourished."

When you are ready, adjust your awareness to the gents and the soft region just below your breast bone. This area is your Solar Plexus; this is the chakra of personal power.

Now, begin to breathe in, and allow your solar plexus to become soft and gently expand your breath. Allow an orange light to wash over you now, providing warmth and comfort, feeling your personal power and self-belief.

Breathe in the refreshing energy that comes with this self-belief. Breathe into your Sacral Chakra- the source of your personal power. Feel this empowered, motivated and strengthened energy. Notice your thoughts without judgment, are they more empowered? Do you feel stronger mentally? Rest in awareness of these thoughts without judging them or feeling the need to change them in any way.

Breath in and breath out, repeat in rhythm and harmony of the movement in your belly. Feel the expansion of your body as you breathe in and breathe out.

Welcome all pleasing feelings and thoughts without judgment, but appreciation for them. Allow them to energize you as you continue the rhythm of your breath.

Allow the orange light to cover and encompass you now. Feel the warmth of this light.

Rest in this awareness as you continue breathing in and out, in the rhythm of calm and relaxation hue noticing your personal power through the Sacral Chakra.

Feel the physical sensations of your body now. Your feet on the floor, your hands in your lap. When you are ready, open your eyes and arise.

## Solar Plexus Meditation (Meditation time approx. 15 when repeated 3 times)

This chakra directly translates to, "lustrous gem." Interestingly, this is the chakra from which your self-belief, confidence and personal power are bred. If you have been a circumstance that was not right for you, or, conversely, a situation where you had a gut feeling that things were going to work out— then you have tapped into the Solar Plexus chakra. Truly, this is your personal power, or solar plexus, at work. You can feel this confidence in physical form within your body, or "gut."

Sit on the edge of a cushion or soft blanket. Form a fist with your right hand and make a cup with your left hand. Now, extend the thumb on your right hand upward. Place the right fist within your open left palm, draw each of your hands right in front of your solar plexus; this is located just elbow your sternum and right above the navel cavity.

Now, close your eyes and connect in a synchronized manner with the rising and falling of your breath.

Imagine that a flame has replaced your right thumb. This flame flickers at the center of your entire being. With every inhale that you initiate, watch this yellow flame grow bigger and brighter. Visualize and feel the warmth that spreads from this region of your body and fills you first from the inside, and outwardly from you. Next, imagine that you've grabbed a small group of sticks. On each and every stick, you will write down a phrase or just a word that represents something within your life that is no longer of service to you. This can be something that you are in the midst of letting go of and removing from your life.

Keep in mind that there are certain things in our life that must be let go of until we are fully free of them, possibly even thousands of times. Forgive yourself during this process, moving on is one of the very hardest activities to engage with.

Stand up, with each of your feet just a little bit wider than the distance of your hips. Reach both of your arms over your head, interweave your fingers, and then extend each of your pointer fingers. When you inhale fresh air into your lungs, reach up high and exhale. Release all of your tension from your spirit. Do this ten times, then pause, the hand being help in a prayer position by your heart, feel the feeling of refreshment within you.

You have connected to your 3rd chakra now; your personal power has been enriched. Repeat this process multiple times to boost your confidence and ensure that you completely move on from whatever is holding you back.

You are able to change. You have the power.

## Solar Plexus (2)

Get yourself into a comfortable position. If you are laying the floor, allow your entire body to fully relax and come into heightened awareness. Leave all of your negative worries and thoughts at the door; this moment is uniquely set out just for you and your personal power.

Acknowledge any sounds that exist inside an outside of the room. Rest in awareness of the room's temperature without judgment. Let all of these thoughts, feelings, and emotions go.

Now, bring all of your soft attention to your solar plexus region. Visualize a beautiful yellow light this light is your Manipura- your personal power and confidence.

How big is this light? Can you feel its energy? Or is it just soft energy? Now allow this light to pass over your entire body and provide warmth with comfort to you. (Repeat these questions in your mind without judgment).

Feel your body becoming more relaxed and embracing feelings of comfort and calm. Your spirit is being strengthened from within as you let go of the past and embrace the new power unleashed within you. Your 3rd chakra, the chakra of your self-belief and personal power is being infused with your spirit.

Bring your attention to your physical sensations now. Start to feel your feet on the floor and hands in your lap. When you are ready, open your eyes and rise.

## Heart Chakra Meditation (Meditation time approx. 15 when repeated 2 times)

This chakra translates directly to "unhurt." This particular chakra is where one's love, kindness, and compassion to themselves and others are found and empowered. This chakra is fairly easy to understand because it is concerned with love in our hearts for others, us, and our circumstances. In this way, this chakra is associated with healing one's pain and instilling health.

Get yourself into a comfortable position. If you are laying on the floor, allow your entire body to relax and become comfortable fully. If you are sitting in a chair, settle your hands on your thighs or at the side of your body.

Now, close your eyes. This time if uniquely set out for you. Leave all of your worries. Let them go.

Have awareness for all of the sounds that surround you; just allow them to be present without judgment or interaction.

Be aware of the shade and light permeating through your eyelids. Feel the soft cool air softly touching your body's surface.

Sense the massive sky above you, along with the broad horizons that stretch around you, feel the earth below you, supporting your weight and body.

Draw in a breath that cleanses you and then breath out all of the tension that has built up inside of your body and mind. Let your breath fall naturally into a rhythm. When thoughts arise, acknowledge them and let them go. You are not a victim of your thoughts. You are a strong and non-judgmental observer. Breathe in and breathe out (repeat with rhythm).

Draw your attention to your chest region. Visualize a beautiful green light in this area, swirling in a circular fashion. How is this light functioning? Is it bright? Is it warm? Is there a tingle associated with this light? What are your thoughts at this moment?

Breathe in this green light all the way down into your hands and arms. Breathe this into your pelvis, toes and legs. Breath this light up into your chest, head, filling the body and connecting with every other chakra inside your spirit.

Now draw your focus to your chest area once again, to the circling green light chakra, notice a small pink rosebud in the very center. Le this pink rosebud unwind slowly, once petal at a time, and opening into a wonderful pink flower that is surrounded by a bright green light with a gold center.

Remind yourself that you are safe once you completely open your heart center to allow yourself to both receive and give others love. Once you breathe this light inward, it will accompany love and openness in your heart. When you breathe out, the green light will diminish all fear within you. Allow yourself to feel the beautiful green glow as it twirls and encompasses you.

Breathing this green light in, and breathing out tension. This is your focus. Repeat to yourself that you are loved and are indeed worthy of love. Breath in, breath out.

It is now time to close this chakra down. Bring all of your attention to your chest, right to the green light that is the Heart Chakra. See the twirling green light decreasing in size. Bring the size of this light down to a small light. Reduce this light to normal function. Repeat the mantra, "My Heart Chakra is operating normally."

Now, bring all of you awareness right back to the consistent flow of your breath. Breathe in and breathe out.

When you feel that you are ready, open your eyes.

## Heart (2)

Find a comfortable seated position. Feel the soft connection of your body to the earth. Rooted to the earth in this way, let your spine drift upwards to the sky, extending to the top of your head. When you inhale, let your shoulders fall from your ears in a gentle manner, allow them to rest softly down your back. Feel the collarbones widen, and your heart opens up.

Now, start watching the subtle flow of life that is breathing through your entire body. You have now become an observer of every way that your body moves you become filled with the force of life.

Now we will start a breathing exercise that will cleanse your nervous system and pride balances all of your body's systems. Start by making a "Peace sign" with your fingers and the place each of the fingertips at the center of the third eye. Next, use your thumb to close your right nostril and then breath deep into your belly through only the left nostril. At the very top of the breath, pause and then close the left nostril and exhale through the right. Allow the inhale and exhale on both sides to be of the exact same length. Use the mantra "I am" when inhaling and "Love" when exhaling.

Now, allow yourself to think of a time when you had received love unconditionally from someone else or when you had given it to another person. Start fostering these feelings that you felt when you were given this love. Whatever emotions manifest, feel them and express gratitude for them.

Allow these feelings to flow into your heart. Now, visualize the center of your heart space and a bright glowing green light.

As this light spins brightly, feel the heart being cleansed of self-doubt, envy and pain toward yourself or others. Release and be cleansed of everything that is no longer serving you. Continue breathing in a harmonious rhythm. Invite these native emotions to be released and accept feelings of peace, joy and passion into each and every one of your cells.

Visualize the roots of these positive emotions flowing to the very root of your spine and into the center of the earth.

Gently begin blinking your eyes as you allow yourself to feel the physical sensations of your feet on the floor and hands in your lap.

Now, open your eyes and rise.

## Throat Chakra Meditation (Meditation time approx. 15 when repeated 3 times)

This chakra translates to "very pure." Notably, the Throat chakra provides a voice to one's personalized truths. Where does one's voice stem from? Where does this energy emirate from? Physically, the answer is clearly the throat. However, as far as your energy is concerned, this energy stems from one's 5th chakra. Indeed, this chakra allows you to express your own truth in a clarified manner.

Get into a comfortable position. You can be seated or lying on the floor, while you let your whole body fall into a peaceful state of relaxation.

Now, close your eyes. Take in a cleansing breath and gently observe the natural rhythm of your breathing. Breathe in and breathe out. Allow thoughts to come and go without judgment. This is your time. Gently repeat the rhythm of your breathing in harmony and serenity.

Bring all of your attention to your throat. Visualize a beautiful small blue light; this light is twirling in a circle.

Observe and accept how this feels without judgment. With every, inhale of air visualize yourself breathing in more blue light. This blue light is filling your Throat Chakra and your neck region, spreading through your entire body and illuminating your spirit. This blue light spreads into your legs and hands. Feelings of relaxation are spreading through you now. This light is connecting with all of your other chakras.


As you inhale, this blue turquoise light provides truth and compassion for listening.
When you exhale, this turquoise blue light will remove everything that is blocking your spirt. All negative

emotions are cast out. This peaceful blue glow spins and encompasses every aspect of you. Remind yourself that your spirit is connected to truth and clarity. Inhale Blue light, exhale tension and inner chaos. Repeat this action.

Now, visualize this blue light, and see it opening in a similar way to a flower. This light stretches far from you but remains connected to your spirit. You will now see the energy and light of positivity and guidance from the Divine that is seeping into you abundantly. Keep this image in your mind for 10 seconds. Count in the rhythm of your breath.

It is not time to close this chakra. Bring all of your attention to your chest region. See the twirling blur light diminishing in size. Repeat to yourself, "My Throat Chakra is operating normally. Its function is normal."

Return all of your power for awareness to the flow of the breath. Breathing in and out in rhythm and harmony. Notice the natural flow of your stomach as you inhale and exhale with every breath.

Bring your attention to your body now. Feel the physical sensations of your body connected to the floor and your hands in your lap.

When you are fully ready, open your eyes and rise.

## Throat (2)

Take a deep breath, extend this breath and then exhale. When you exhale, shift all of your attention to your throat. Visualize a blue light glowing as your chakra. This chakra now spreads in a vibrating harmony, like a pulse, from your throat to fully fill your neck and head. Now it moves to fill the rest of your body.

Imagine that you are strolling through a forest on a very small path. This pathway is lined on each side by massive trees that offer shade from the sun. Now, you can hear the sounds of small bugs and animals moving around. Birds are chirping as well. Far in this distance, a gentle stream flows over a rock bed and is making a soft flowing sound.

You now come across a narrow clearing that sits along with a huge log with a brush covered floor. You stroll next to it and sit down with your back gently against the log.

The forest's sounds are clearer in this position. These sounds carry a special meaning and you are able to hear them along with sounds that are fainter. This entire forest is playing music just for you.

Your fifth chakra is twirling and building its strength within you. It starts to spin faster; a gentle blue light starts to wash over your body and enters every cell and every single pore within the body.

Take a deep breath, and allow yourself to fully feel the energy that funnels through your throat, which is burning with a bright blue light.

Rest in this awareness. Now, stand up and begin walking from the log that has fallen at the very edge of the forest. This is where you first started. Take a gaze back at the forest that is signing just for you.

When you feel fully ready, open up your eyes and rise.

## Third Eye Chakra Meditation (Meditation time approx. 15 when repeated 2 times)

This chakra translates to "beyond wisdom." The function of this chakra is to open your mind to information that is beyond simply the material world and your 5 senses. Enhanced sensory perception, intuition and or psychic energy are all derived from the 3rd eye. There is a small land in your eye that is shaped much like a pinecone that takes light in. This gland is called the pineal gland and is responsible for helping you feel awake in during the day and tired at nightfall. Ancient cultures, far before modern brain imaging, were privy to the existence of the third eye, realizing that it receives information from sources that are outside of our 5 senses.

Find a place where you are completely comfortable and will not be disturbed. Wear loose or unrestrictive clothing and turn down the lighting if it is too bright.

Start with a deep inhale and breathe through your nose. Hold this for a short period and then release it gently through the mouth. When you do this, feel a sense of relaxation to come over you.

Let go of thoughts that enter your mind that heighten fear and doubt about yourself and others. Inhale through the nose and exhale through the mouth. When you exhale, let go of fears that exist within your mind.

This process is natural and very safe. The gold light will place you in a more polished frequency where there are only positive experiences. Now, relax and let these experiences happen.

Let the golden circle of light within your forehead to completely open and send gentle rays of light in every direction. Let this light relax you fully.

Allow your body to fall into more relaxation. Further into relaxation with every breath.

Feel that your body is becoming light, your weight is decreasing, and you will fall into a state of relaxation. More light will begin to flow right into your third eye and all throughout your entire body.

Completely let go of all uncertainty. All questions of doubt are released into the atmosphere and fully released from you with every breath.

Allow yourself to open your third eye in a natural way... now you will relax in a complete way... feeling more and more relaxed as the golden light of the third eye flows out from your forehead.

## Third eye (2)

For this meditation, there will be 24 steps split into 3 days for added benefit and to aid your grasp of the benefits that it has to offer.

Find a place where you are completely comfortable and will not be disturbed. Wear loose or unrestrictive clothing and turn down the lighting if it is too bright.

This third eye meditation will progress slowly and provide ample time for you to settle in and enjoy the experience.

Start with a deep inhale and breathe through your nose. Hold this for a short period and then release it gently through the mouth. When you do this, feel a sense of relaxation to come over you.

Allow your face to fully relax, unclenching your jaw and letting all of the muscles in your face to relax.

With this, your body will soon to begin to relax as well. You may feel a sense of warmth coming over you.

Welcome this relaxation to spread over your entire body and increasing as it moves more deeply through you.

Bring all of your attention right between your eyebrows. Rest in awareness of your Third Eye. This is the energy within the forehead, this radiates and opens light. Visualize a gentle image of light nearly the size of a golf ball that radiates gold light similar to the sun. This light will radiate in all directions around you.

Steady your breath and visually this light surrounding you from your Center. Repeat this over and over until you feel the warmth completely encompass you. Repeat this process 10 times. Feel this energy around you.

When you are ready, open your eyes and rise.

## Crown Chakra Meditation (Meditation time approx. 10 when repeated 3 times)

This chakra can be translated to, "thousand petaled." As such, this chakra is the energy of pure consciousness. Moreover, this chakra is a noticeable difficult energy to fully explain in a manner that is not convoluted or interwoven with pedantic syntax. Think of this energy as analogous to magnetism. The color of this chakra is violet-white, and its Center is found at the very top of the head. The energy of this chakra radiates between one's eyes, extending in an infinite manner outward and upward, and then connecting you to the rest of the universe's energy.

If you can, hike all the way to the summit of a particular place, this can be a mountain, a roof, etc.) Bring a blanket, flowers, and possible matches and a candle as well. The goal here is to create a sacred space for yourself.

Peacefully place your blanket on the ground, and put the altar together as you contemplate the meaning that all of these items have to you.

Take up a cross-legged seat on top of your blanket. Now, put your left hand over the heart area on your chest. Gently place your right fingertips on the ground beside you.

Close your eyes and fall into a natural comfort into your seated position. Feel your deep connection to the earth. Let you back, and spine rise with the top of your head rise to the sky.

Now, connect to the natural flow of your breath. Allow yourself to feel the special value of this connection immediately.

Feel each falling and rising of your body with each breath. Every breath comes and goes, experience this fully. Rest in the awareness of the belief that there is a life force that is breathing in and out of you. Something deeper than you that resides within you.

This very force is giving you all of the breath that is needed to maintain your life. This force is within and around your entire existence. This force is everything, everything beyond your body and your life.

Open yourself to the possibility of being connected to this force. You can name this spirit anything you wish: God, Life, Mother...

Recognize the presence at this moment. Embrace its energy.

When you are ready, take one last deep breath. Open your eyes and rise into the rest of your day.

## Body Scan (10 mins. Repeat 5x)

Feel your feet rested comfortably on the floor.

Feel the cold air inhaled through your nostrils

Notice any unique bodily sensations that you are feeling

When you are distracted or lost in thought, bring your attention right back to your breath

Feel the rise and fall of your chest as you inhale and exhale

Feel and notice where the movement of your breath is felt in your body

Notice the influx of thoughts and then return to a bodily sensation or the breath

Notice where your body is uneasy or uncomfortable

Notice whether your breaths are shallow or deep without changing them

Move continually from the top of your head down to the soles of your feet

Allow the pain and discomfort to pass through your body and let it go.

**Finally, if you found this book useful in any way, a review is always appreciated!**

www.ingramcontent.com/pod-product-compliance
Lightning Source LLC
Chambersburg PA
CBHW060408080526
44583CB00012B/504